Liam's Big Heart

Story by Diane Forti
Illustrations by Carter Stuart

Copyright © 2022 by Diane Forti

No part of this book may be reproduced in any form or by any electronic or mechanical means, or the facilitation thereof, including information storage and retrieval systems, without permission in writing from the publisher, except in the case of brief quotations published in articles and reviews. Any educational institution wishing to photocopy part or all of the work for classroom use, or individual researchers who would like to obtain permission to reprint the work for educational purposes, should contact the publisher.

ISBN: 979-8-218-01103-1
LCCN: 2022909694

Printed in the United States of America

Dedicated to: Maney, the best and most lovable dog EVER!

And to: Liam; thank you for sharing your Big Heart for the whole wide world to enjoy.

Love, Dede

There once was a little boy named Liam. He was the youngest child in the Preddy household. His oldest sibling, Brookey, was twelve and a super sweet big sister. She always made sure Liam was included in their fun games and treated him like a person and not like a five-year-old little kid.

Liam's big brother, Jimmy, was nine and also extra good to him . . . well, most of the time. The two boys had their fair share of wrestling matches, which usually ended up in a bump on the head or a rug-burned elbow. Jimmy was a star soccer player and enjoyed teaching his younger brother fancy footwork skills! Overall, Liam was a happy, typical kindergartener—or so his parents thought.

Liam absolutely loved animals and was constantly bringing all types of furry critters home that had gotten injured. One time, he found a rabbit that evidently got his ear torn in a jagged fence, and then there was a squirrel that got his bushy tail halfway chewed off by the mean neighborhood cat. The local veterinarian, Vet Matt, was always curious to know how Liam found these hurt animals.

Liam's mom was usually happy to help out, but she drew the line when Liam brought home a four-foot-long snake! "But he has a bellyache," said Liam, very convincingly.

"And just how do you know that, mister?" his mother asked, standing at a safe distance.

"I just know," said Liam with a shrug, and with this simple explanation, Liam's mom mumbled something about this being a job for her husband and off she scooted. She was grateful for her son's special bond with God's creatures . . . most of the time.

But Liam was different in other ways too. He had been born with his right leg three inches shorter than his left and a tiny hole in his heart. The doctor said that the hole would probably close on its own as Liam grew older but that he shouldn't overexert himself. There was nothing to do for his short leg except to wear an elevated shoe so he wouldn't be off-balance.

Liam's parents tried not to be overprotective of their youngest son. They prayed every day and night for the safety of all of their children, but what they prayed for the hardest was that Liam wouldn't need heart surgery. This was a frightening thought, so they left this dilemma in God's hands. Liam's mom said that His hands were a lot stronger than theirs.

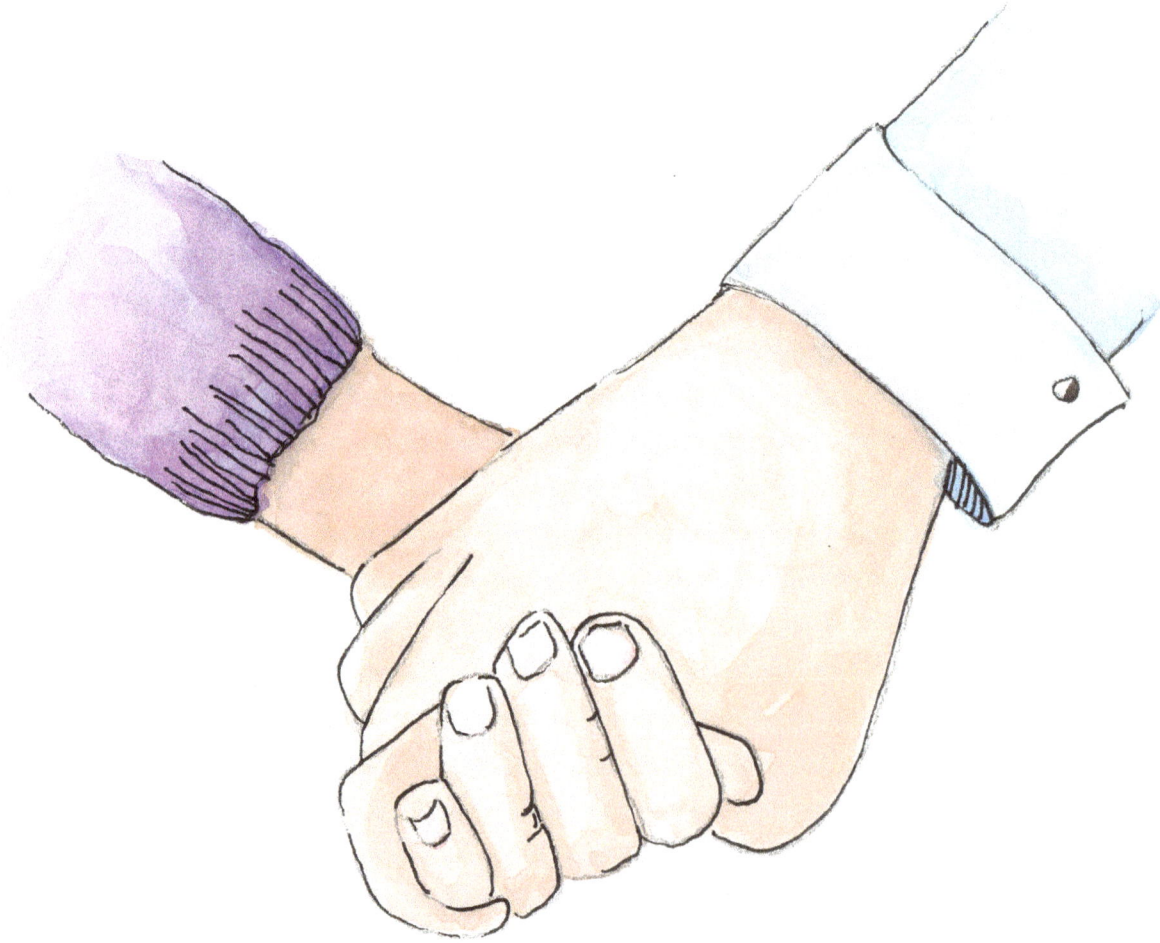

    As summer was approaching, the older kids were invited to an amusement park for an end-of-the-school-year party. But Liam wasn't allowed to go; he was simply not old enough. Before he could plead his case to his parents, his mother's cell phone rang. It was Dede, Liam's grandmother, calling for him. "If you're not too busy, I need your help with our new rescue German shepherd. We are going to the lake for a month, but Maney is old and needs special attention. Would you like to join us and help out?" she asked Liam.

    "With you, Gampa Ken, and a dog . . . for a whole month?!" exclaimed Liam. So, it was settled, and Liam didn't think twice about missing the school party. He was so excited to have his grandparents all to himself—and, of course, the new dog friend too.

Before Liam's dad dropped him off, he made Liam pinky swear that he wouldn't whine about what Dede fixed for meals. Liam was the pickiest eater ever! "Yes, sir. I promise, I promise, Daddy!" And with a quick kiss and hug, Liam scurried up to his grandparents' house. Out of breath, he busted through the front door and stopped dead in his tracks. There, in front of him, was the biggest, most handsome dog that he had ever seen!

Liam dropped to his knees up close to Maney, gently stroked his head, and introduced himself. Liam told Gampa that he thought Maney looked sad, and Gampa explained that Maney's owner was too old and sick to take care of him any longer. Gampa Ken had seen the dog posted on the SPCA website and just had to rescue him, and Dede agreed.

Dede had already taken Maney to Vet Matt, and he explained that Maney was very old and slowing way down; in dog years, he was almost a hundred years old! But the veterinarian had some suggestions for keeping him healthy, like changing his dog food and taking him on slow, short walks. Liam didn't mind this at all because sometimes his special shoe was like a heavy weight that made him feel tired. So, they were a perfect match!

Gampa, Liam, and Maney went out for a walk. Liam noticed that Maney didn't bark or wag his tail. The tips of his ears were droopy. He didn't give any of the trees or bushes a good sniff. And the bossy lake cat just pranced in front of Maney without him even looking her way. "I've never seen a dog totally ignore a cat before," said Liam with a perplexed expression. "Maybe he doesn't feel well, or he's sad," he guessed.

"Well then, hug him gently and talk to him," said Gampa. "Isn't that what your parents do when you're feeling a bit down?" So, Liam did exactly what his grandfather suggested, little by little.

Gampa Ken and Liam set up a tent behind the cabin and were going to sleep outside, like a real camping trip! Liam was busy picking up sticks for a campfire while Maney flopped in the middle of the yard and supervised. Liam stopped every few minutes to pat Maney's head and tell him about all the injured creatures he had rescued and how he imagined they had gotten hurt.

Liam included Maney in his conversation as if the dog understood every word. "I think he is smiling just a little, and his tongue is hanging out too," Liam said to his grandfather.

"That's a good sign for sure. Now if you can get him to eat, that would be a miracle!" Gampa said enthusiastically.

Liam and Maney went inside to take a break from the heat. Dede turned on Liam's favorite movie and served up a cool drink for both of the hardworking fellas. Maney lay on his side, and Liam used his thick fur as a pillow. Before too long, an hour had passed without any movement.

Dede returned from the store and witnessed this precious picture; an old dog and a little boy resting comfortably without a care in the world. Dede saw four sleepy eyes begin to open, and Liam said in a quiet voice, "I hear Maney's heartbeat going lub-dub, lub-dub, but then I hear a fluttering sound."

Dede said that Vet Matt had already checked Maney for heartworms, but Liam politely interrupted his grandmother and said, "Yes, but what if he has a different kind of heart problem? Like me. Can't dogs have problems with their hearts like people do?"

Dede pondered this question from her inquisitive grandson and agreed that Vet Matt would know the answer, so off to see the good doc they went!

"You are exactly right, Liam," said Vet Matt as he put his stethoscope up to Maney's chest. "It sounds like Maney has an irregular heartbeat, and it may be the reason he isn't feeling well. I think it can be corrected with some medication, but you have to make sure he gets a dose every day and keep walking him, without fail," Vet Matt said, sounding very stern but also kind. He loved animals, too, just like Liam. "You probably saved his life, Liam," said Vet Matt.

Maney seemed to understand and licked the side of Liam's face over and over, as if to say "Thank you." Liam was overcome with happiness but didn't know what to say, so he hugged Maney around his neck and didn't let go for quite a while. He felt pure joy in his heart, like the feeling of Christmas morning!

    After getting Maney's medicine, the trio headed back to the lake. Gampa had everything set up for their camping night and was even starting to roast hot dogs and veggie packs over the fire. Maney's nose twitched as he sniffed his new food, but he wasn't interested in eating it. "I think he wants a hot dog," said Liam.

    "I've never met a dog that would refuse a hot dog," chuckled Gampa. So, Dede pulled apart a cooked wiener and mixed it into Maney's food.

    Over dinner, Gampa entertained them with a story about space aliens and pirates and buried treasures. Gampa had been telling this story to his grandchildren since they were little, and he added more to it every time they were together.

    Liam was all ears, listening while he ate his hot dog, and Dede just rolled her eyes lovingly at them both. That was when she peeked over at Maney . . . and saw him eating his food!

    Liam exclaimed, "He's eating, he's eating!"

    His grandparents said in unison, "And so are you!"

    Dede said that this called for an "after dinner" blessing! So, they held hands, Liam put his hand on Maney's paw, and they thanked God for their delicious food and their awesome new dog.

That night, Maney slept at the tent's opening, as he was their official watchdog, and the family felt very safe with him there. Dede woke up in the middle of the night and found that Maney had moved inside the tent to lay next to his little boy. Liam's arm was draped over Maney's back, and it was a God-given, beautiful sight. Now if only God could answer their prayers of healing Liam's heart. This was a blessing they were counting on.

The next day, Gampa Ken and Liam decided to go canoeing. "But Maney wants to come too," Liam said in his usual convincing manner. Gampa joked that Liam would make a good lawyer, but Liam said that he was going to be a veterinarian like Vet Matt! They all put on their life jackets. Gampa was even able to strap Brookey's vest onto Maney. Gampa instructed, "Absolutely no standing up in the canoe, boys!"

It was such a pretty day. The lake's calm water was a blue-green color and as smooth as shiny glass. Gampa and Liam were usually very talkative, but they were quiet today, and the only sound they heard was

Maney's panting. Gampa pointed out several fish that jumped out of the water right in front of the canoe. The fish were putting on an acrobatic show for them!

They paddled around for a long while and had just started heading back when Liam spotted a mother duck with her ducklings. Liam wasn't the only one who saw the ducks. Just then, Maney jumped up and started barking like a hunting dog! "Maney, sit! Sit, boy!" yelled Gampa, but it was too late.

Maney leapt up onto the dock, causing the boat to rock back and forth wildly and then flip over! As if in slow motion, Liam and Gampa tumbled backward into the lake. When they bobbed back up in their life jackets, they saw Maney above them on the dock, dry as a bone and barking playfully at them. "Maney!" they both shouted in unison.

Maney jumped into the water like he was a young pup again and doggy paddled over to join in their fun. "Crazy dog," said Gampa, shaking his head.

Liam added, "I don't think Maney thinks he's a dog at all. He's like a person with fur—a real member of our family!" With this profound statement, the three fellas continued to splash and swim. Liam was having the time of his life! He couldn't wait to tell Brookey and Jimmy all about it! But he did miss them, and he thought that Maney probably missed his previous owner too.

At dinnertime, Liam told Dede all about their exciting day! Without thinking about it, this once picky eater was eating sweet corn on the cob, oven-fried chicken, and Dede's famous smashed potatoes!

Maney was lapping up his dinner, too, and didn't notice that Liam had crushed up his heart medicine and mixed it into his food. Liam was determined to help his new buddy feel better!

As the lazy days and weeks of summer came and went, each day was filled with a funny Maney story, and Liam was his ever-present companion. Now when they went walking, Maney gave each shrub a thorough inspection with his powerful sniffer, his ears perfectly perked up like a trained police dog. He even showed that prancy lake cat who the real boss was! The grandparents noticed that both Maney and Liam were able to walk farther than either could on their own without getting tired. Dede was sure that Liam had grown at least an inch since coming to stay.

One evening, as they were finishing dinner, Maney, with a full belly, laid down next to Liam's feet, perfectly content. "You know," said Dede, "I think that God sent Maney to us so that you could help him. And . . . I have faith that Maney has patched up the little hole in your heart."

"When am I gonna be able to see Maney again?" Liam asked, realizing that he would be returning home soon.

Dede held Liam's sweet face in her hands and said, "I promise that you can see Maney as much as your big heart desires." And with that vow, they made plans for gatherings after church on Sundays to include all of their family members. Liam had told Vet Matt that he would help care for his new best friend, and he would always be true to that promise.

About the Author

Diane Forti has been a registered nurse for thirty-two years, specializing in urology and hospice. Diane and her husband, Ken, have a combined family including twelve grandchildren whom they are very close to. She is the author of two other children's books, *Pinky Swear* and *The Very Nice Family*. In her next writings, she is exploring works to include young teens in *No Matter What*.

About the Illustrator

Carter Stuart is a Virginia native who received her Bachelor of Fine Arts in both graphic design and painting/drawing from Anderson University in South Carolina. She has illustrated several children's picture books, whose titles include *Higgins Takes Flight*, *Garden Tales: A Seed's Story*, and *What's that Smell, Mommy?* Along with creating whimsical illustrations for children's literature, she also enjoys portraiture and watercolor.

www.ingramcontent.com/pod-product-compliance
Lightning Source LLC
LaVergne TN
LVHW072123060526
838201LV00068B/4958